Fresh Start

Farm-to-Table   Plant-Based Baby Recipes

by Erika Krebs

edited by Anne Pici

ISBN-13: 978-0615872612
ISBN-10: 0615872611
Fresh Start Publishing

Dear Anna—

Enjoy !

Erika Krebs

2

DEDICATION

I would like to dedicate this book to:

My amazing husband, Michael, for always telling me I can do anything. He will have my heart forever.

Mom continuing to love me even though she didn't live to see our beautiful children. I miss her every single day.

Dad for taking us to the farms and always supporting my crazy ideas.

My sister, Kisty Riley, for teaching me you can learn to cook at any age.

Laury Falter for all her incredible advice.

Nikki Leatherbury Cerra and Anne Huter Chandra for always putting up with me.

Ann Pici for editing because she knows Mom would have done the same.

Barbara Farrelly for always being straightforward with me.

Hidden Valley Farms for allowing me to take pictures and show them off.

My sons, Oliver and Sebastian, for being my inspiration.

Our newest addition, Phoebe Joyce, who will be another adorable taste tester!

Table of Contents

Special Notes

I am an official Community Leader for First Lady Michelle Obama's Let's Move Initiative. This program works with Choose My Plate. The MyPlate image is a visual guide to daily nutrient requirements. Each recipe includes a MyPlate image featuring the key ingredients' food groups. For more information, please visit ChooseMyPlate.gov

All Recipes are free of:
Peanuts
Meat
Dairy/Lactose
Egg
Added Salt
Added Sugar

freshstartcookbook.com

Introduction

I will never forget when our pediatrician said, "Congratulations, your babies are now old enough to start solids. Easiest way is to start on rice cereal and then transition into pureeing **the foods YOU eat**."

REALLY? The foods **I** eat? It was definitely an "ah-ha" moment! It was one thing for me to indulge in pizza, burgers, and steak. But was I REALLY going to feed such things to my babies? No way. I looked at my twin boys as a **Fresh Start**. They had never been introduced to salt, sugar, processed foods, refined foods, and fast foods - all those things that were basically my diet!

Unfortunately, a chicken nugget these days is NOT the same as the chicken quality we were fed when we were little. There is little nutrition in nuggets and other such food — not to mention the lack of compassion in raising the chickens in the first place, as well as the whole environmental impact of getting that nugget to your baby's plate. In fact, the whole process behind a chicken nugget made me rethink how I approach food, starting with reflecting on my own history with nutrition.

I was born and raised in a small town in Ohio and ate a typical Midwest diet. My father's side of the family didn't grow up with much so they saved money by purchasing fruits and vegetables directly from farmers. When I was a child, every year my dad would purchase half a cow from a local farmer (who also happened to be our plumber!), and we would freeze the steaks we got from our side of the cow. Dad would also take us every fall to the farms to get huge pickles straight out of the barrel and to pick up lots of ears of corn — nothing better in the world than fresh corn! I went back last summer to one of the farms where we'd gone, Hidden Valley Farms, and the barrel of pickles was still there - here is the picture to prove it!

My mother's side of the family had a similar financial situation but a very different eating lifestyle. I have many memories of going to the grocery with my maternal grandmother to buy canned meat and logs of processed American cheese because … well, because that was what the government provided. To save money she would also cook her eggs in reused sausage lard, and I ate a lot of canned succotash. Growing up, my sister and I also ate a lot of the standard comfort foods: meat loaf, mashed potatoes, green bean casseroles, biscuits and gravy, etc. Don't get me wrong — all were absolutely delicious. However, looking back, I'm in shock that I haven't had a heart attack yet.

After college, I moved west and lived in California for fifteen years. This had a huge influence on my diet. I was surrounded by people who focused on foods so different from those in my upbringing. California was my introduction to foods such as mangoes, avocados, kiwis, and sushi. And then, of course, getting pregnant changed my views about food still further. Eating fast food several times a week just didn't seem like the right start to creating life.

I decided to eat a lot less processed food, and meat. And thankfully my cravings were for oranges. Lots of them. I would eat eight to ten of the little Cutie oranges A DAY, and in the last trimester I drank about a quart of orange juice on top of the Cuties. (Yes, I also got four cavities from all the citric acid). I also will be the first one to admit that I still partake in a few gluttonous acts of  processed foods, and I've learned how much our eating is about habit. I will spend the rest of my life probably fighting periodic cravings for unhealthy foods.

After having our twins, I realized what an amazing opportunity I had to make an impact on their health. And it's not that I want to raise my children in a bubble in which they are never allowed certain foods. However, since they are "starting from scratch," they have no idea what being addicted to salt and sugar is like. I have a chance to control their diet for at least the first few years of their lives. It might seem hard for you to turn away from serving cake and cookies and instead serve fruits for dessert. However, in my mind, it seems to be an easier decision than having to control their diet after the fact if they were to become Type 2 diabetic. I have to keep reminding myself that my boys have no idea what they are missing. When they go off to school and are introduced to processed foods, I can only hope that they have been given a chance to understand good nutritional values — and to make better eating decisions based on a few years' worth of habit.

It's important to know that a plant-based diet is often misunderstood. I get mixed reactions from people when I tell them what my children eat (or don't eat). Most people are incredibly supportive, excited, or just plain curious. In fact, most of my friends now ask for my recipes and are interested in receiving sample batches as I hunt for more "taste testers." What I find frustrating is the handful of people who judge, rather than try to understand, my plant-based diet choices for my children.

One of my goals with this cookbook is to share a handy resource of great and proven plant-based recipes for those interested in a Fresh Start with their children. Another is to educate those who haven't had the time or inclination to do as much homework as I have on what they are putting in their babies' mouths and bodies. There are enough recipes out there that focus on unhealthy ingredients, so I am just trying to balance the cookbook world out a bit!

"I alone cannot change the world, but I can cast a stone across the waters to create many ripples."

Mother Teresa

The recipes in this book have significant nutritional value and will help babies and toddlers develop a well-rounded palate that is so essential to establishing their preferences for vegetables, fruits, and other "superfoods" important for proper growth and development. Given the health issues plaguing our children—from obesity to Type 2 diabetes — it's imperative that parents introduce infants to nourishing, high-quality foods from the outset because doing so will help shape children's food preferences and, ideally, have a positive impact for life.

I hope my book helps you on this path by providing you with delectable, straightforward recipes that are perfect for growing healthy babies and toddlers. No matter which recipes you prepare, I promise each offers taste, nutrition, simplicity, and enjoyment.

So — take out your blender, feeding spoon, and baby bib, and get ready for a fun-filled adventure with your little one. There are many tasty memories ahead!

Chapter One

Why a Plant-Based Diet?

Raising my children on an organic plant-based diet is one way I can directly and actively contribute to their future — their future health and their future environment most obviously. But I also feel that this diet will teach them a lesson in compassion for animals. I hope that any one of these reasons is motivation enough for you to want the same for your children.

All traditions start somewhere. Let this one start with you.

Eating Organic

Everything I put in my babies' mouths is organic. I believe it is critical in this day and age to purchase organic for you, and even more critical for your babies.

I'm not buying organic because the food has more nutrition. I'm buying the $.99-a-pound banana versus the $.79-a-pound banana because I am hedging my bets that 6 billion pounds of pesticide a year might actually have a negative impact on my children's bodies. Until there is a study that proves that a chemically treated red apple is just as safe as a chemical free apple, investing in the latter works best for me and my peace of mind. So, in order to keep at least some chemicals out of the air, water, soil – and out of our babies' bodies – invest in organic. It's not worth possibly finding out down the road what the long-term negative effects are of all the pesticides.

Organic is not only about our health, but also about the environment. Industrial agriculture pours pesticides and synthetic fertilizers on it's soil, which goes into our waters. It then affects the environment downstream and becomes a major contributor to dead zones in our ocean environments. As best said by ecologist Aldo Leopold, "A good farm must be one where the native flora and fauna have lost acreage without losing their existence." This is exactly what we find at an organic farm rather than at an industrialized commercial farm.

"If we are going to live so intimately with these chemicals — eating and drinking them, taking them into the very marrow of our bones — we had better know something about their nature and their power."

Rachel Carson
American marine biologist and conservationist in her 1962 book Silent Spring

With that said, **assume that every ingredient listed in this book is organic**. If I wrote the word *organic* before each ingredient, this book might be twice as long! So, as you bring your tote to your local farmer's market or grocery, please ask someone if a product is organic, or look for the USDA Certified Organic symbol:

For more information, please visit:
http://www.ams.usda.gov/AMSv1.0/NOPConsumers

Eating for Your Health

I would never compromise my children's health in order to succeed in some moral agenda. In fact, it's quite the opposite. And since a plant-based diet is often misunderstood, I made sure that I went to a nutritionist to confirm that my boys were getting all the right nutrients, something that I would strongly recommend to anyone interested in health, plant-based or not.

Here's how it started. When my babies started eating solids, they were around six months old. I began documenting everything they ate, including amounts, mostly because one child had allergies and I was trying to narrow down the culprits. It was when they were eight months old that I took them and my two months' food schedule to the nutritionist. She also had an entire blood panel done so she could further evaluate anything that they might be low on.

Well, my boys got a shiny gold star of approval. In fact, my nutritionist said that I was welcome to feed her kids any day – and that I should create a cookbook. Hmmm...what a great idea! But the main idea for ensuring the best nutrition for your children, is first, to talk to your pediatrician and/or nutritionist so that you are working together.

Following a healthy, balanced, plant-based diet ensures a host of health benefits. Take a look. All of the following nutritional benefits come from a plant-based diet full of foods such as fresh fruits and vegetables, whole grains, nuts, beans and soy products. This is an impressive list, and learning to talk the talk of nutrition helps you take ownership of your children's health.

1. **Reduced Saturated Fats.** Dairy products and meats contain a large amount of saturated fats. By reducing saturated fats in your children's diet, you'll improve their current and future health tremendously, especially cardiovascular health.
2. **Carbohydrates.** Carbohydrates provide energy for your children. They are a necessity. When they don't have enough carbohydrates, their bodies will burn muscle tissue, so grains, a main source of carbohydrates, are absolutely needed!
3. **Fiber.** A diet high in fiber (something plant-based eating usually guarantees) leads to healthier bowel movements and helps fight against colon cancer.
4. **Magnesium.** Aiding in the absorption of calcium, magnesium is often overlooked as a vitamin needed in a healthy diet. Nuts, seeds, and dark leafy greens are an excellent source of magnesium.
5. **Folate.** This B vitamin is another important part of a healthy diet. Folate helps with cell repair, generating red and white blood cells, and metabolizing amino acids.
6. **Potassium.** Potassium balances water and acidity in your body and stimulates the kidneys to get rid of toxins. Diets high in potassium have been shown to reduce the risk of heart diseases and cancer.
7. **Vitamin C.** Besides boosting the immune system, vitamin C also helps bruises heal faster and keeps your gums healthy.
8. **Antioxidants.** For protection against cell damage, antioxidants are one of the best ways to help our children's bodies. Antioxidants work by interacting and stabilizing free radicals, or unstable molecules in the body.
9. **Phytochemicals.** Plant-based foods provide phytochemicals, which work with antioxidants to possibly prevent many diseases and boost protective enzymes.
10. **Protein.** We all know children need protein, but it maybe be surprising to learn that most of them eat too much and usually in the wrong forms, such as red meat and chicken nuggets. A much healthier way to get the right amount of protein in a plant-based diet is with beans, nuts, peas, lentils, and soy.

Did you know?

Broccoli has 11.1 grams of protein per 100 calories while the steak has 6.4 grams of protein per 100 calories. That's almost twice the amount of protein!

Disease Prevention

If that list isn't enough to convince you, there's more. Eating a healthy plant-based diet can also prevent a number of diseases. Find out from the list below what you could potentially avoid for your children just by switching to a plant way of eating:

1. **Type 2 diabetes.** A plant-based diet is a weapon against Type 2 diabetes. Type 2 is usually adult onset diabetes with poor diet as one of many contributors to the cause. This is not to be confused with Type 1 Juvenile Diabetes that has no causes due to poor diet. A plant-based diet is also easier to follow than the standard diet recommended by the American Diabetic Association. None of these recipes call for sugar except what is found in natural foods. Most people have heard that Americans consume way too much sugar, which could possibly lead to Type 2 diabetes. Relying on other sweeteners that are not synthetic, processed, or derived from animal products is a healthier way to eat. Many plant-based diets do not contain much processed sugar because most cane sugar is refined through activated charcoal, most of which comes from animal bones.

2. **Blood Pressure.** A diet rich in whole grains is beneficial to our health in many ways, including avoiding high blood pressure.

3. **Cholesterol.** Eliminate any food that comes from an animal, and your children's hearts will thank you.

4. **Prostate Cancer.** Studies have shown that men in the early stages of prostate cancer who switched to a plant-based diet can possibly slow the progress of the cancer. Starting your child on this type of diet now is considered preventative medicine.

5. **Colon Cancer.** Eating a diet consisting of whole grains, along with fresh fruits and vegetables, can really reduce your child's odds of getting colon cancer.

6. **Breast Cancer.** Countries where women eat very little meat and animal products have a much lower rate of breast cancer than countries where women consume more animal products. Another preventative reason for starting your children on a plant-based diet now!

7. **Heart Disease.** Eating more nuts and whole grains, while also eliminating dairy products and meat, will improve cardiovascular health. Plant-based diets are extremely beneficial in preventing heart attacks and strokes.

8. **Macular Degeneration.** Diets with lots of fresh fruits and vegetables, especially leafy greens, pumpkin, carrots, and sweet potatoes, can help prevent the onset of macular degeneration. Think of your child's eyesight now.

9. **Osteoporosis.** Bone health depends on a balance of neither too much nor too little protein, plus enough calcium intake, high potassium, and low sodium. In a plant-based diet, all four of these points set a perfect scenario for preventing osteoporosis.

10. **Arthritis.** Eliminating dairy consumption has been connected to alleviating arthritis symptoms. Having a plant-based diet is promising for preventing rheumatoid arthritis.

11. **Allergies.** The human body is not designed to digest cow's milk and cow's milk dairy products, yet the idea of milk being healthy is pushed in this country. Dairy is the number one allergy in children, followed by eggs. This is a really important reason for me to instill a plant-based diet with my children since one of my sons, Oliver, is allergic to egg whites.

Eating for the Environment

I always considered myself "earth friendly." I recycled my beer bottles, you know? I asked for only one napkin at fast food chains, and I replaced our toilets with low-flush systems. I'm doing more than the average person, right? But who wants to be average? Is this the planet I want to leave for my children, and is this how I want to teach my children to treat the Earth? I realized I had to do more. After much research I realized that one of the most responsible lessons I can teach my children is to eat a local, organic, plant-based diet. Eating a plant-based diet is more environmentally efficient because it greatly reduces the wastes, pollution, and deforestation caused by mass raising of animals.

Global meat consumption is highly concentrated. The United States and China, which together contain 25 percent of the world's population, combine to consume 35 percent of the world's beef, over half of the world's poultry, and 65 percent of the world's pork. If Brazil and the European Union are included in this group— roughly 33 percent of the world's population—it consumes more than 60 percent of the world's beef, more than 70 percent of the world's poultry, and more than 80 percent of the world's pork.

ACCORDING TO THE USDA, THE AVERAGE AMERICAN CONSUMES NEARLY TWICE HIS OR HER WEIGHT IN MEAT EACH YEAR.

IF YOU WEIGH 150 POUNDS, THAT WOULD BE LIKE EATING AN ENTIRE 300 POUND HOG A YEAR.

Today, our planet is home to nearly 1 billion pigs, 1.3 billion cows, 1.8 billion sheep and goats, and 13.5 billion chickens—more than two chickens for each man, woman, and child on the planet. We have altered vast ecosystems and devoted massive resources to support the world's burgeoning livestock herds. These animals need to be fed. They need water to survive. If they are ranged, they need land. And these animals produce enormous quantities of waste.

The ecological footprint of meat production is deep and wide, and ranges from forest destruction in Central and South America for ranching to suppression of native predators and competitors in the United States. Nearly one-quarter of the world's meat, primarily beef and mutton, depends on a natural ecosystem: rangelands. Yet, as overgrazing becomes the norm in much of the world, rangelands are being pushed beyond their limits.

DID YOU KNOW?

"It has been estimated that one 50,000-acre hog farm can produce more waste than the entire city of Los Angeles" OrganicConsumers.org

According to the Environmental Protection Agency, the world's livestock herds are the largest source of human-induced emissions of methane—a potent greenhouse gas contributing to climate change. In the United States, where 130 times more animal manure is produced than human waste—5 tons for every U.S. citizen—animal waste is the principal source of water pollution. And livestock farms are getting larger throughout the world. For those concerned about our environment, reducing meat consumption is as fundamental as reducing car use or being a conscientious recycler.

Eating with Compassion

I grew up in the Midwest, where meat is not just a staple but a requirement. If you did not have an animal protein on your plate, then it wasn't a real meal, it was an appetizer! However, after moving to California and opening my diet to a more plant-focused environment, I realized that I don't need a chunk of dead animal on my plate to call it a meal.

Compassion for humans

Seven pounds of grain are required to produce one pound of beef; the conversion is 4-to-1 for pork and 2-to-1 for poultry. Each pound of meat represents several pounds of grain that could be consumed directly by humans, not to mention the water and farmland required for growing the grain. In layman's terms, the beef in a hamburger represents enough wheat to produce five loaves of bread.

Huge amounts of food — not to mention the water and farmland required for growing the food — can be freed up by modest reduction in meat production. Just think: 98% of the U.S. soybean crop is used for livestock feed, and 49% of the total maize harvest is used for livestock feed.

If each American reduced meat consumption by just 5 percent, roughly equivalent to eating one less dish of meat each week, enough grain would be saved to feed 25 million people—the number estimated to go hungry in the United States each day.

Did you know?

If the 670 million tons of the world's grain that is now fed to livestock were reduced by 10 percent, the resulting grain could feed 225 million people or keep up with growth in the human population over the next three years. - Brian Halweil, a researcher at the Worldwatch Institute

Compassion for animals

When I grew up in Ohio, our family would purchase half a cow from the local farmer, keeping the meat from our side of the cow in the deep freezer. We had meat for the year. But for many people, times have changed. And attitudes. If you ever want an eye-opening experience about where your meat comes from now, just Google these two words: "factory farming." Then you'll know how the majority of meat is currently produced.

The process to get that steak on your plate has not just included taking the life of an animal for now it's never giving them a real life to begin with.

In these modern factory farms, animals are routinely injected with hormones and stimulants to make them grow bigger and faster. Feedlots are crowded, filthy places with open sewers and choking air. The animals would not survive at all but for the fact that they are fed huge amounts of antibiotics. In some farms, cattle are fed "renders" - dead and ground-up cows. Similarly, to induce and increase egg production, chickens are kept in tight cages and kept awake under bright light 24 hours a day.

The cruelty behind that cheeseburger is simply no longer how I want to teach my children about animals and food. I am starting fresh with my children and teaching them a compassionate relationship with animals, making sure they know that animals are their friends not their food. Care to join me?

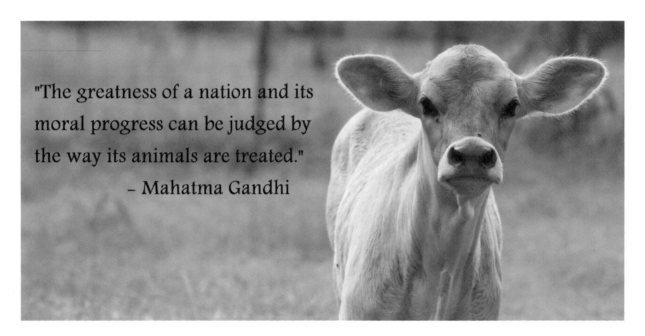

"The greatness of a nation and its moral progress can be judged by the way its animals are treated."
– Mahatma Gandhi

Chapter Two

Nutrition 101

According to the American Dietetic Association (ADA), "appropriately planned vegetarian diets, including total vegetarian or vegan diets, are healthful, nutritionally adequate and may provide health benefits in the prevention and treatment of certain diseases. Well-planned vegetarian diets are appropriate for individuals during all stages of the life-cycle including pregnancy, lactation, infancy, childhood and adolescence and for athletes."

Good nutrition is critical for the growth and development of your child during the first two years. When you feed your children a proper diet, you are: starting them off with a healthy advantage I n the world, helping the environment, and showing your children compassionate morals. The goal is to instill a positive and healthy attitude towards food, towards self, and towards others.

During those first two years, however, your child's feeding needs change drastically. A baby goes from drinking only breast milk or formula, to drinking thicker liquid food, to swallowing purees, to learning to chew with no teeth, and then to chewing with teeth. It's a radical change to undergo, and keeping up with the texture of food called for is just as demanding as delivering an adequate amount and variety of essential nutrients.

Because your child's first two years is a period of astounding and rapid growth, nutrient requirements per pound of body weight are proportionally higher than at any other time in the life cycle. That's an impressive situation—and a humbling one for mothers to contemplate. Although there are numerous nutrients needed for humans, only a limited number of these have been included in the USDA requirements.

Nutrition Assessment

In order to determine your child's specific nutritional needs, it is critical for you to have a nutritional assessment provided by either a certified nutritionist or your pediatrician.

For example, while my sons don't eat meat, it was very important to meet with a nutritionist to set up a healthy action plan so they could get their protein fulfillment. This was made even more challenging because one son is allergic to peanuts, egg whites, and walnuts, limiting him even more.

And while the United States Department of Agriculture (USDA) provides Dietary Guidelines for Americans—most recently updated in 2010—these guidelines only start at the age of two. For children under the age of two, the USDA provides general Dietary Reference Intakes (DRIs), which are based on the nutrient content of foods consumed by healthy infants with normal growth patterns.

So, just as I am providing a guideline of nutritional requirements according to the USDA, you might still have to customize a diet since each baby is unique. Infants differ in their body size, growth rates, medical history or problems, and physical activity levels. I am providing simply a guideline of the basic nutritional needs that you can use to plan your meals for your baby more accurately—and to discuss with your nutritionist or pediatrician. Their expertise becomes even more important if a child's diet demands particular attention.

Calorie count?

Here is an easy rule to start with: **Unless your baby has special needs, don't count your baby's calories.** If you are providing a substantial healthy diet, such as the recipes in this book, let your child's always-changing situations lead the way here. A baby's calorie requirements vary drastically because of physical activity, genetic factors, medical conditions, body size, etc. As long as your child gets regular checkups with a pediatrician, and as long as growth falls within normal PERCENTAGES, then the best generic thing you can do is simply feed your child until he or she is no longer hungry. And believe me, a child will let you know! For example, a baby will just turn his head away from the food, or she will push the spoon away with her hand, or he will refuse to open his mouth. A child might even fling the food—especially if he knows you have just cleaned the floors!

Choose MyPlate

The USDA used to provide a food pyramid for people to have an easy visual reference as to how much of each food group they needed in their diets. But this pyramid's proportions changed over the years, and so now there is a much easier identifier called MyPlate. MyPlate is an easier-to-read illustration of the five food groups and portion sizes.

As you prepare your baby's food, keep this image in mind. While many of these recipes are purees, think about what ingredients are in the puree and how they can be broken down onto the MyPlate. If there is a missing food group in a puree, look for another recipe that has that and serve as a side dish or as another meal in the same day. This way your child can meet all their nutritional needs. I have used this icon for each recipe as a guide for you to more easily track your baby's daily nutritional requirements.

With a typical diet, it's easy to think protein means meat and dairy means milk. That's all I knew growing up in Ohio. However, with a plant-based diet, there are some great alternatives:

The **Dairy** food group is important because it provides calcium, vitamin D, protein, and potassium. The most familiar examples are cow-based milk, cheese, and yogurt. But there are so many substitute plant-based products that offer these very vitamins and minerals, including milk, cheese, and yogurt - instead made from **soy**, **almonds**, **tofu**, **coconuts**, and **rice** .

The **Protein** food group is important because it provides not only protein, but also iron, zinc, Omega-3s, and B vitamins. While the protein group I grew up on was **meat**, **poultry**, and **fish**, this group also includes such super providers as **dry beans**, **peas**, **nuts**, and **seeds**, which are actually much better for your heart because they don't have as high cholesterol levels.

Basic Nutrients

Plant-based diets can include eating a limited amount of meats, a vegetarian diet, and a vegan diet. I created the recipes in this cookbook, however, to be completely vegan because, while you may choose to feed your child limited meats and/or dairy, there are enough cookbooks out there to help you with those recipes.

If you choose to raise your baby on a plant-based diet, you must make sure that you have some basic knowledge of nutrition in order to ensure your baby will be fed a proper diet that includes all dietary needs. To ensure you provide a well-rounded diet for your baby, you must find sources other than meat or dairy for protein, B-12, calcium, vitamin D, zinc, iron, and Omega-3 fatty acids. While many of these nutrients are found in meat, understand that your baby can definitely get all his nutrient needs met from other sources. Here are some ideas for alternatives:

Protein is necessary for the growth and maintaining of body tissue. There are plenty of examples of plant sources, such as **legumes**, **soy, nuts, peas,** and **seeds**.

Vitamin B-12 is needed to produce red blood cells and maintain nerve function. Examples of alternative sources are fortified **soy products**, **nutritional yeast**, and **fortified unsweetened breakfast cereals**.

Calcium is needed for strong teeth and bones. Examples of alternative sources are **dark green vegetables**, **almonds**, **red** and **white beans**, **tofu made with calcium sulfate**, and **calcium fortified foods or drinks**.

Vitamin D helps the body absorb calcium. Since Vitamin D is not found in most plant foods, the best alternative examples are **fortified foods** or a **supplement.** The labels on many soy or almond milks proudly proclaim that they are Vitamin D fortified. I give my boys **liquid vitamin D drops** in their food for extra help, as recommended by my pediatrician.

Zinc has many needs in body functions, including immune response, brain function, and reproduction. Examples of alternative zinc sources are **nuts**, many types of **beans** (such as **white beans**, **kidney beans**, and **chickpeas), soy products**, **pumpkin seeds**, **wheat germ**, and **whole grain breads**.

Iron helps many functions in our body, including the carrying of oxygen from our lungs to the rest of our body and the digesting of food. Admittedly, plant-sourced iron is not absorbed by the body as easily as meat-sourced iron. Therefore, if you are considering a plant-focused diet, you will have a higher requirement of iron than a meat-focused diet. Examples of alternative sources include **soybeans**, **tofu**, **tempeh**, **legumes**, **spinach**, **kidney beans**, **black-eyed peas**, **peas**, **whole wheat breads**, and **fortified cereals**. Also, iron is more easily absorbed when paired with foods rich in Vitamin C.

Omega-3 fatty acids are vital for healthy heart and brain function. Some alternatives can be found in **walnuts**, **canola oil**, **soy**, and **flaxseed**. However, a different type of Omega-3 fatty acid known as **DHA** can be found in **supplements** and **fortified foods**.

You'll become a pro at identifying these foods once you get a fresh start in this book, but to help the learning curve, I suggest Food-a-Pedia, a great website for looking up the nutritional breakdown of over 8,000 foods. https://www.supertracker.usda.gov/foodapedia.aspx

Chapter Three

Introduction to Solids

It felt like just yesterday that my babies were born, but then one day here they were ready to sit in chairs and eat solids. They really grow way too fast! Going into this parenting thing, I had absolutely no direction, and not to feel sorry for myself, (ok, just a little), my mom had recently passed away, so no traditional help there. Also, we had moved to a new city when I was six months pregnant, so that meant there was nobody nearby whom I could call.

I did, though, have a friend, Nikki Leatherbury Cerra, who visited me when the boys were about two months old. I remember one morning in particular, when we made oatmeal together. I poured my usual six tablespoons of brown sugar in my serving, thinking I was healthy because it was BROWN sugar! But Nikki proceeded to put chopped cranberries in the bowl for her 18-month-old daughter. I was blown away that a child would eat what I considered plain oats--blech! To top it off, Nikki then cut open an avocado and spooned it directly into her child's mouth. And to top THAT off, her child couldn't eat enough of it. At the time, I didn't appreciate exactly how great this diet was for Nikki's daughter. I think I just chalked it up to "hippie food."

So when my boys were ready for solids, I still hadn't come to the full realization of how much my culinary world would have to change. I armed myself with a baby food book I received from another Nikki friend, Nikki Drake, and my studying started. Ok—rice cereal? Check. Now, on to the infamous oatmeal. I had to stop in my tracks and think about the sugar. Can sugar hit you like a ton of bricks? I had flashbacks to my pediatrician's saying "For your boys, purée for them foods that you eat." But if that was the case, was I really going to put six spoonfuls of sugar in their oatmeal? Suddenly brown sugar didn't seem all that healthy. And so the journey to healthy food began....

Is your baby ready? Are you ready?

Some babies are ready to start eating solids as early as four months, but most are starting to show signs of interest around their six-months mark. But make absolutely sure that you consult with your pediatrician first. I tried feeding my boys at six months, but Sebastian was not really getting the swallowing motion well and so spit everything out. I waited about three weeks more and tried it again, this time with success. Since each baby's development is different, here are some signs to look for in yours:

- He has good head control and can sit up alone or with support.
- He is showing more interest in food. For example, he might watch you eat a bit more intently, open his mouth when he sees food, or even reach for your food.
- He can use his lips and tongue to do the swallowing motion rather than spit it out.

The first food I fed my boys was rice cereal. I originally questioned why rice because it didn't seem to have much nutritional value. But the reason is that babies are still getting the majority of their nutrition at this age from their breast milk or formula. Rice cereal, while not holding much nutrition, is easy on their bellies and has been shown to cause very few allergic reactions. I think you have enough on your plate already—getting your baby used to sitting in a highchair, making sure he or she doesn't instantly pull the bib off (Seriously, why are most of them Velcro?), etc.— so dealing with an allergic reaction should be last on your list. In other words, stick with something basic. There has been recent news that rice could possibly have a high level of arsenic in it. If you are in question, go with the baby barley cereal or oatmeal as a starter.

I purchased bulk brown rice, which is so common now you can find it in most grocery stores. Just make sure it's organic. You can add formula or breast milk to it also, which makes for an easier transition for your baby since he or she is already familiar with this taste.

Feeding your baby

When?

You can feed your baby at <u>any</u> time of day. Certainly you can try feeding them when you know they are hungry. Begin with a few spoonfuls of cereal, and then give them breast milk or formula. However, my boys would get cranky if not fed what they were used to, and the new stuff was a bit overwhelming for them. So in the very beginning I fed my boys as more of a "fun activity," and then once they got over the excitement of sitting in a chair, wanting to play with the spoon, etc., I simply started feeding them when they were hungry.

How?

Most important, to prevent choking, make sure that your baby is sitting up. Of course, be completely prepared with towels because there WILL be a mess. I let my boys touch their food so they can use all their senses. Did I mention this gets messy? No need to let them fling it, but just dip their fingers in it a bit. Feel free to skip this if you want, but somehow I liked the idea of making food tactile.

I used a baby spoon and ate the first bite myself to show them (another reason to make your own food—ever tried canned peas? Nasty.). Talk to your baby, too, explaining how yummy this new thing is and making sure to show excitement on your face—yes, even when you think it's the blandest food on the planet and wish you had your stash of brown sugar on hand.

Look for the swallowing motion. Oliver got it right away, but Sebastian would either let the cereal drool out of his mouth, or his tongue would push it out. Give it a couple tries, and if the drooling still happens, give your baby a few days or even a week, and then try again.

Also look for signs that your baby is finished eating. I think most babies are alike in this category: they will lean away from the food, push it away with their hands, close their mouths, or start fussing. Or all the above. Again, don't get too frustrated that you went to all the effort to make this food, get the bib on, get him or her in the chair, put on the drama about the awesome taste . . . all for two bites. Plus, if you aren't producing much breast milk, I would not waste too much of it in the cereal because a lot of it will go to waste.

In the beginning your child will probably eat only a few bites. Completely normal. Remember, this is all entirely new to him/her. It took my boys about three weeks to build up to eating about half a cup. But then once they did, I started on the oatmeal and barley cereal. And no, I did NOT put any sugar in it. Babies are, as I called this book, a Fresh Start. They have not been exposed to sugars and processed foods, so there is absolutely no need to add sugar to anything in their diet. If you keep this in mind throughout your whole food journey, it becomes easier to keep it basic. While as adults we still might need to dip our fruit in chocolate, there is enough sugar in a strawberry to fulfill your baby's sweet tooth.

Advancing to Purées

When your baby gets the knack of eating and swallowing, he or she is ready for puréed solids. I started my boys when they were almost seven months old. Being a mother of a child with allergies, though, I can't emphasize enough the importance of introducing only one new food at a time, and waiting two to three days before starting another.

After each new food, watch for allergic reactions, such as diarrhea, rash, vomiting, hives, or eczema. If any of these occur, stop feeding the new food and consult with your pediatrician as soon as possible. <u>Always</u> consult with your pediatrician, and with an allergist if necessary, regarding introducing solids so that you're working as a team.

The very first puréed foods I found the easiest were vegetables like sweet potatoes and carrots because they purée to a very smooth texture and are very low-allergenic. I've also read that some people don't give fruits right away because they are so sweet. It's your choice, but I think sweet potatoes are just as sweet as pears and apples anyway. Up to you. If you are having a tough time with your baby not completely accepting solid food, you can add breast milk or formula to add the comfort of a familiar taste. I did only vegetables for the first couple of weeks just because, again, they purée so smoothly, not because they are less sweet. I did hold off a bit on citrus fruits for Oliver because he has eczema and he would turn very red around the mouth area after eating them. But citrus fruits were just fine for Sebastian. Again, consult with your pediatrician or allergist.

Did you know?

If your baby eats the mass produced commercial baby food at the rate of three jars a day, you will be recycling 540 glass jars before he or she reaches his or her first birthday!

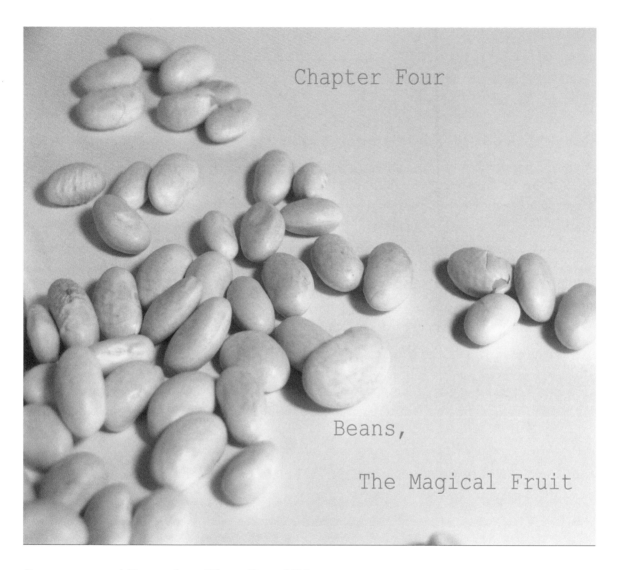

Chapter Four

Beans,

The Magical Fruit

Importance of Beans in a Plant-Based Diet

Hey, they're so important they get their own chapter! Beans are so loaded with nutrition, where do I begin? Only green vegetables come as close as a valuable food source. Beans are simply loaded with protein and fiber, and they are low on the glycemic index, which measures how quickly blood sugar levels rise after eating a particular kind of food.

Thanks to our super-sized-food nation, we have a grossly exaggerated concept of how much protein we need to consume on a daily basis. It is so ingrained in our culture that most of us feel we need some sort of meat at every meal. Not true. We actually need only a fraction of the amount of protein most of us regularly consume. For example, mother's milk, the ultimate perfect food, contains only 1.6 grams of protein per ½ cup, which is less than half the amount of protein in cow's milk. As soon as a baby turns one parents are told to switch to cow's milk. What's wrong with this advice? The greatest growth spurt in our lives is when we are babies, so if we needed that much protein to grow, why wouldn't it be found in breast milk?

If that's not enough, there are also risks to eating too much protein. If we eat too much protein, it is broken down by the kidneys, which in turn damages the kidneys from overwork and wears down their filtering system.

So, yes, we need protein – but not a huge amount of it. A variety of plants foods provide all the protein we need. So, my best advice is to stick to plants and make a plan with your pediatrician or nutritionist.

This brings me to more great news – how great beans are for your blood sugar levels. Foods are rated on a glycemic index (GI) to indicate how quickly their natural sugars are released into the bloodstream. **The lower the GI number, the slower the release and the better the food.** Beans are super heroes here. For example, kidney beans are a 29 on the GI. Compare that 29 to jelly bean's high GI of 80. Hence, that's why we feel a sugar high from jelly beans, then a crash, and then another hunger spike soon after.

It's also hard to ignore the importance of fiber in beans. Fiber is important because it cleans out the digestive tract **and** it helps break down fat **and** it helps keep cholesterol low. If your family has a history of high cholesterol, it is that much more important to teach your baby a plant-based diet!

Did you know? A quarter-pound burger has ZERO fiber,
while one cup of pinto beans has 14 grams!

With our babies now getting a fresh start to the world regarding nutrition, beans are critical in establishing healthy food tastes. I am so thrilled that my children now coo when I pull out a bowl of lima beans as a snack. This snack gives them enough protein and fiber, and it keeps them full longer.

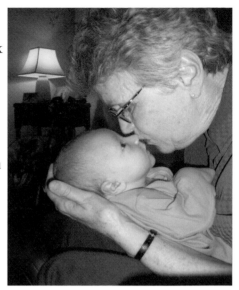

With this picture of Mom, I think there's no better time in this book to incorporate a tune called "Beans, the Musical Fruit." It's a tune my mother sang to us at dinner describing the importance of beans and fiber: "Beans, beans, the magical fruit. The more you eat, the more you toot. The more you toot, the better you feel. So let's eat beans at every meal." And yes, I now sing this to my boys too. Thanks, Mom!

Bean Storage

So now that you are on board with the importance of beans, you might want to know how you get them and how you store them? Of course any local grocery store will have canned beans, and these are great if you are in a rush because they are already cooked and ready-to-serve. Other than that, though, I strongly recommend buying beans in bulk (ie. dried beans) instead. Canned beans are a lot more expensive, they are canned in aluminum (think BPA), they contain salt even if you get a low-sodium variety, and they are not as good for the environment. A can weighs more, so it takes more fuel to get it to the store and then to your home, and then you still have the can to recycle - which requires more energy - or the can ends up in a landfill.

In contrast to canned beans, dried beans are cheaper, healthier, and more eco-friendly. A triple plus! I first bought the dried beans because they were so much less expensive. My outlay for bean protein is about $1.89 a pound—versus organic canned beans at around $3.00 a can, or meats that run anywhere from $5.99 to $24.99 a pound. My boys were starting to eat like horses, and I just knew I had to buy in bulk. An added bonus is I don't have to worry about the can, and because I freeze extra, when I'm in a rush I can simply warm some up.

I store my beans in extra-large Mason jars because they stay reliably sealed and so are fresh for a long time. I actually keep the Mason jars of dried beans, lentils, and grains out on my counter because I love the beautiful decor they provide.

Preparing and Cooking Instructions

But what are you supposed to *do* with those dried beans? Beautiful as they are in Mason jars, they're like little pebbles, and a lot of people simply aren't familiar with how to get them from the Mason jar or bag to the table. First, relax. Dealing with dried beans might seem intimidating, but the process is actually really easy. It requires time, but not really much effort.

1. You need to pick through them. Beans are an agricultural product, so there will be rotten beans in the mix. Throw away any shriveled up beans or broken ones.
2. Next, rinse them off in a strainer to remove any dust.
3. Pour the beans into a BIG pot and fill the pot with cold water to three times the amount of volume.
4. Soak overnight, anywhere from eight to fourteen hours. You <u>can</u> skip this step and simply boil the beans right away, but boiling actually takes a lot longer—and I don't think they taste as good as beans that get an overnight rest.
5. The next morning, drain the beans and then rinse them again in a strainer. Put them back in the large pot, and this time add enough water to cover the beans by about two inches. Do <u>not</u> add salt.
6. Bring the beans to a boil, and then simmer over low heat for 60 to 90 minutes or until the beans are tender.

And here are some portion tips:

One pound of dried beans is equivalent to about 4 cans of beans.
7 cups of cooked beans are equivalent to about 4 cans of beans.

I will measure out whatever amount of beans immediately after cooking the entire batch. Then I let the beans cool and dry, freezing the leftover beans either in a Mason jar or in a bread bag tied with the rubber bands that came with the bread loaf.

If life is being normal for us and I'm actually planning ahead, I will take the frozen beans out the night before I use them so they are ready for the next day. Unfortunately, I don't always plan ahead, so most of the time I will take a handful out and either heat them up in a pan for the recipe I need them for, or defrost them in the microwave for a finger-food snack.

Here are my Cliff Notes for this chapter:

Eat beans.
They are good for ya. (and because *I* said so)!
Sort, rinse, soak, boil, freeze!

An anthropologist proposed a game to children of an African tribe. He put a basket of fruit near a tree and told the kids that the first one to reach the basket would win all the fruit. But when he told them to run, they all took each other's hands and ran together, then sat together enjoying the fruits. When asked why they ran together like that, as one could have taken all the fruit for himself, they said "Ubuntu. How can one of us be happy if all the others are sad?" Ubuntu is a philosophy of African tribes that can be summed up as "I am because we are."

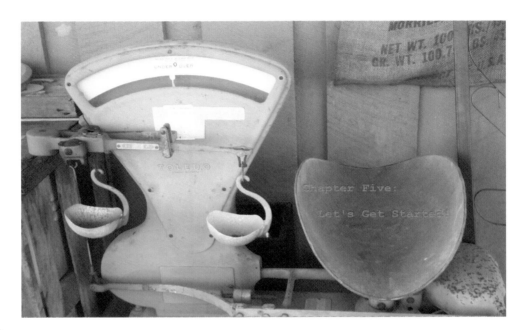

Basic Supplies

To start the whole baby food process, I invested in the following tools:

Blender

All you really need is any blender, but don't tell my husband that! I confess I'm a kitchen supply snob, so I got the crazy expensive VitaMix. It's truly my best friend in the puree world because it probably has more horsepower than my car. It can liquify an apple. I pull this blender out (I call it my "big guns") when I'm preparing lots of food to freeze. But I repeat: All you really need is any blender.

Mini Food Chopper

I prefer a mini rather than a large food processor only because this is the tool that I use the most out of all. If I'm blending/mashing a banana, I don't need to use a huge blender – more cleaning. And a mini food chopper is so much easier to handle. Unless you really are feeding an army, this should be easier to manage.

Knives

I like using three different knives: a chef knife, a paring knife, and a serrated knife. The chef knife has just a basic 8- or 9-inch blade, which is good for cutting larger foods, such as pineapples. It's great for chopping and dicing. The paring knife is the same thing, just a smaller version, usually a 3- or 4-inch blade. This is good for prepping smaller foods, such as figs or strawberries. The serrated knife can be any length, but I've found a 5-inch blade works well. This knife is perfect not only for cutting bread, but also for any food that has a skin to cut through, such as a tomato.

Utensils

I cook with only stainless steel or wood utensils, steering clear of plastic. A handy oversized spoon, a slotted spoon, a spatula, and tongs are my everyday necessities. I love my silicone spatula because it's easy to clean and is flexible to really scrape everything out of the bowl.

Kitchen Towels

You can never have enough kitchen towels. I keep an entire drawer full of kitchen towels because I am almost as messy as my babies in the kitchen! I have some fun towels that I keep out seasonally; I particularly love my Halloween ones, as do the twins. But I also stock up on my yucky towels, the ones I don't care about getting stained – like the ones I use to clean up blueberry juice. I really like using flour-sack towels for cooking because they are thin enough for wiping a little tomato juice off my cutting board before I cut something else, and they are nice and large. Then I like my super absorbent towels for when I spill milk everywhere and for drying dishes. When any towel has outlived its life in the kitchen, it gets retired to the garage and is used as a household rag. As I'm writing this, I'm starting to wonder if I have a bit of a towel obsession because I could really keep going...

Ice Cube Trays

Ice cube trays offer perfect portions for freezing your purees. Each cube is approximately 1-2 ounces, depending on the tray brand. If you have to measure exact amounts of foods for your baby, measure your tray's capacity by pouring water into one cube division, then pouring it out into a liquid measuring cup.

Freezer Containers

At first, you can separate your cubes into different containers, but after awhile you can throw them all together in one large container. I can tell you that I have developed a strangely keen eye for telling the difference between pureed frozen cubes of peas, spinach, pears, or kale!

Mason Jars

The ice cube trays are great for small portions, especially when you are feeding at home. For example, you can just grab two or three cubes from the freezer, nuke them for about one minute, stir, and voila.

But if you know you are going to be out and about, small pre-filled Mason jars are great. They come in all sizes, including jars as small as 4 ounces, equivalent to a typical store-bought baby food jar. In fact, this is when it is really easy to see how much money you save: Compare how many cubes or jars you have to the cost of a pre-filled store-bought jar. It adds up!

You can freeze the wide-mouth canning jars – a real plus – but make sure you read the packaging label when you purchase them. Look for the words *wide mouth* and *freezer safe*. If you don't find these words on a package, you run the risk of the glass cracking as the water in the food expands. I pass along this tip speaking from experience! Also, don't fill the jars all the way to the top; leave some space for expansion. When you choose what jar of frozen food you would like to feed your baby, transfer it from the freezer to the fridge so that it can be ready for the next day. Mason jars are also perfect for canning your baby food if you know the canning process – another book for another day!

Bowls and Spoons

Make sure to stock up on lots of bowls and spoons. It's good to have plenty on hand so that you aren't running your dishwasher half empty to get more dishes or getting stuck hand washing dishes over and over. I bought silicone-coated baby spoons for my boys when they first learned to eat because they were soft on the gums. When they turned a year old, I purchased bigger silicon-coated spoons for warm food since the spoons don't get hot. I also have lots of small stainless steel spoons that came with my silverware set. My guess is they are supposed to be for coffee stirring or something, but they make great baby-size spoons. Sometimes being creative and finding things you might already have is a great option not only for saving some money, but also for saving the environment by reusing.

Pots and Pans

A few years ago, I went crazy and stocked my kitchen with every size pot, pan, and skillet. Guess how many I use now? About three. Have a good stock pot, at least 8 quarts; a good skillet, at least 10 inches (I prefer 14, but then, I have twins); and a good sauce pan, about 3 quarts.

Staple Foods

Here are the food items that I keep stocked at all times in my kitchen. I use them constantly.

Grains
8-grain cereal
steel-cut oatmeal
quinoa
barley
whole grain farro
whole wheat bread
wild rice

Fruits and Vegetables
apples
avocados
bananas
pears
sweet potatoes
tomatoes
broccoli
spinach

Oils
extra virgin olive oil
coconut oil
walnut oil
sesame oil

Legumes /Nuts/Protein
kidney beans
white northern beans
black beans
pinto beans
red lentils
green lentils
edamame
tofu

"Dairy"
 soy or almond milk
soy or almond yogurt

Conversion Tables

Americans typically measure ingredients by volume, while just about everyone else measures them by weight. Here is a quick summary of some of the basic cooking conversions. I wonder if some day we'll all be on the same page.

US Dry Volume Measurements

Measure	Equivalent
1/16 teaspoon	dash
1/8 teaspoon	a pinch
3 teaspoons	1 tablespoon
1/8 cup	2 tablespoons
1/4 cup	4 tablespoons
1/2 cup	8 tablespoons
3/4 cup	12 tablespoons
1 cup	16 tablespoons
1 pound	16 ounces

US Liquid Volume Measurements

Measure	Equivalent
8 fluid ounces	1 cup
1 pint	2 cups
1 quart	2 pints
1 gallon	4 quarts

US to Metric Conversions

Measure	Equivalent
1/5 teaspoon	1 ml
1 teaspoon	5 ml
1 tablespoon	15 ml
1 fluid ounce	30 ml
1/5 cup	50 ml
1 cup	240 ml
2 cups (1 pint)	470 ml
4 cups (1 quart)	.95 liters
4 quarts (1 gallon)	3.8 liters
1 ounce	28 grams

Oven Temperature Conversions

Fahrenheit	Celsius
275°	140°
300°	150°
325°	165°
350°	180°
375°	190°
400°	200°
425°	220°
450°	230°
475°	240°

Weekly Menu for Babies 6 to 12 Months Old

Your baby should be fed at least three to four times a day, and remember to stick to purees only until they are ready for the next step. Along with these meals, your young baby should also probably still be receiving a minimum of 18 ounces of breast milk or formula a day. I recommend a breakfast, lunch, dinner, and nighttime meal. I found this was especially true when my boys were around 6 to 8 months old. Since they weren't eating huge meals, I would give them an 8-ounce bottle after breakfast and another after lunch. They would then get a last 8-ounce bottle in the evening before bed. My boys went through phases of hunger, so some days they would polish off all 24 ounces, and some days they would drink only 16 ounces. I have put together one week's menu for you to follow. You can make the foods ahead of time and freeze them so that you can really stretch this menu across a few weeks. Of course, the bottles of milk listed in the following menus can be substituted by actual breast milk.

Day 1	**Day 2**
Breakfast: Basic Apple Cinnamon Oatmeal p. 66 bottle of milk	Breakfast: Peach Blueberry Tofu Mash p. 96 bottle of milk
Lunch: Chickpea Puree p. 85 Simply Avocado p. 60 bottle of milk	Lunch: Rosemary Carrot Puree p. 75 Homemade Applesauce p. 59 bottle of milk
Dinner: Broccoli, Peas, and Pears Puree p. 64 Simply Banana p. 60	Dinner: Banana, Strawberry, and Brown Rice Puree p. 86
Nighttime Snack: Leftover Basic Apple Cinnamon Oatmeal	Nighttime Snack: leftover Peach Blueberry Tofu Mash

Day 3

Breakfast:
Baby Barley Cereal p. 57
Simply Banana   p. 60
bottle of milk

Lunch:
Mashed Cauliflower Potato Puree p. 70
bottle of milk

Dinner:
Turnip Cauliflower Puree   p. 72
Simply Avocado   p. 60

Nighttime Snack:
leftover Baby Barley Cereal
bottle of milk

Day 5

Breakfast:
Peas, Pear, and Spinach Puree   p. 91
bottle of milk

Lunch:
Beet and Sweet Potato Puree   p. 76
bottle of milk

Dinner:
Cauliflower Lentil Puree   p. 93

Nighttime Snack:
leftover Peas, Pear, and Spinach Puree
bottle of milk

Day 4

Breakfast:
Banana Walnut Cereal p. 106
bottle of milk

Lunch:
Beet and Sweet Potato Puree   p. 76
bottle of milk

Dinner:
Chia Seed Puddin' p. 99
Simply Banana p. 60

Nighttime Snack:
 leftover Banana Walnut Cereal
 bottle of milk

Day 6	**Day 7**
Breakfast:	Breakfast:
Strawberry Rhubarb Quinoa Puree p. 102	Crockpot 8 Grain Cereal p. 69
bottle of milk	bottle of milk
Lunch:	Lunch:
Creamy Corn p. 63	Green Peach Smoothie p. 94
bottle of milk	bottle of milk
Dinner:	Dinner:
Cauliflower, Leek, and Bean Puree p. 78	Chia Seed and Banana Puree p. 108
Nighttime Snack:	Nighttime Snack:
leftover Strawberry Rhubarb Quinoa Puree	leftover Crockpot 8 Grain Cereal
bottle of milk	bottle of milk

Weekly Menus for Babies 12 to 24 Months Old

Right around when they turned a year old, my boys' appetite increased ten-fold! I found I was cooking differently than I was the first six months. The first six months was about learning new foods, learning what they like, being creative, and freezing my purees in ice-cube portions. By the time the boys hit twelve months, I felt more like an army cook. I would spend my Sundays making mass recipes and freezing them in mason jars instead of ice trays because the cubes were just appetizers now. Remember also that I have twins, so everything had to be doubled. Note that I don't put portion sizes on any of my recipes because all babies are different and eat different amounts. Even my twins are very different. They will go through phases in which Oliver will eat an entire bowl of oatmeal, while Sebastian will only want two bites of a banana, and then the next day Sebastian will eat like a horse, and Oliver will nitpick his food. So, no portion sizes here—sorry!

Also at this stage of life, my boys loved finger foods. So I would stick to a few recipes a day. It got a bit easier to feed them because finger foods are so basic! Here is a one week menus that includes finger foods. Again, make extra and you can repeat this another week without much time in the kitchen!

Day 1	**Day 2**
Breakfast:	Breakfast:
Crockpot 8 Grain Hot Cereal p. 69	Cherry Apple Puree p. 88
banana cut into small bites	bottle of milk
bottle of milk	
Lunch:	Lunch:
Farro with Edamame, Peas, and Mushrooms p.132	Split Pea and Sweet Potato Mash p. 117
peach, cut into small bites	boiled edamame as finger food
bottle of milk	bottle of milk
Dinner:	Dinner:
Squash Spaghetti p. 122	Avocado, Beans, and Rice p. 121
avocado slices	orange cut into small bites
Nighttime Snack:	Nighttime Snack:
leftover Crockpot 8 Grain Cereal	leftover Cherry Apple Puree

Day 3

Breakfast:
Cranberry Almond Wheat Berries p. 135
bottle of milk

Lunch:
Butternut Squash Puree p. 100
boiled edamame as finger food
bottle of milk

Dinner:
Beans 'n Rice p. 112
watermelon, cut into small bites

Nighttime Snack:
leftover Cranberry Almond Wheat Berries

Day 4

Breakfast:
Cherry Quinoa p. 118
bottle of milk

Lunch:
Peach Blueberry Tofu Mash p. 96
nori (seaweed)
bottle of milk

Dinner:
Pasta Marinara p. 114
Homemade Applesauce p.59

Nighttime Snack:
leftover Cherry Quinoa

Day 5

Breakfast:
Black Bean and Sweet Potato Scramble p. 128
bottle of milk

Lunch:
Banana, Strawberry, and Brown Rice Puree p. 86
bottle of milk

Dinner:
Potato Leek Puree p. 80

Nighttime Snack:
leftover Black Bean and Sweet Potato Scramble

Day 6	Day 7
Breakfast: Banana Walnut Cereal p. 106 bottle of milk	**Breakfast:** Peach Blueberry Tofu Mash p. 96 bottle of milk
Lunch: Cranberry Edamame Couscous p. 125 bottle of milk	**Lunch:** Quinoa Stir Fry p. 130 bottle of milk
Dinner: Split Pea and Sweet Potato Mash p. 117	**Dinner:** Squash Spaghetti p. 122
Nighttime Snack: leftover Banana Walnut Cereal	**Nighttime Snack:** leftover Peach Blueberry Tofu Mash

Sample Snacks

Since you will be putting time and effort into preparing most of these recipes for your baby's meals, it's nice to have some easy "go to" snacks that you don't have to spend much time preparing. If I'm out running errands, I will usually pack a banana, an avocado with a spoon, and a bento box full of beans and seaweed. I know, seaweed sounds strange, but it's high in protein and fiber! Here's a list of great options for other snack foods.

cooked carrots
cooked asparagus
any soft fruit cut into bite-size pieces:
      very ripe pear, orange, fig, watermelon, oranges, peaches, raspberries, blackberries, blueberries
yogurt – soy, almond, or coconut
banana
nori (dried seaweed)
tofu cubes
sweet peas
hummus and bread chunks
any plain boiled bean:
      lima, white northern, pinto, black, edamame, etc.

Chapter Six

Recipes

Beginner Purées:
6 - 12 months

Beginner Rice Cereal

Ingredients
1 cup brown rice
2 1/2 cups water

Put both rice and water into a small pot and bring to a boil. Reduce heat to low, cover, and simmer for 50 minutes. Turn off heat and keep covered, allowing rice to "steam" for another 10 minutes.

Purée to a smooth texture, adding in formula or breast milk to thin if necessary.

Serve warm.

One of the first foods you can give a baby is brown rice cereal. It's a perfect first food because it's mild tasting, low allergy tolerance, and easy to digest. I recommend using breast milk or formula instead of alternative milk because your baby is already familiar with the taste.

The only time that I had eaten barley was in soup and I thought it was pretty yummy! But then I did some homework and learned that barley contains eight essential amino acids. So now I know that barley is yummy AND it's good for you! In fact, eating whole-grain barley can regulate blood sugar, reducing the blood glucose response to a meal, for up to ten hours after consumption.

Barley Baby Cereal

Ingredients

1 cup ground barley
4 cups water

Bring liquid to a boil, add the barley, and simmer for 40-50 minutes, stirring occasionally. You want to overcook the barley so that it's really soft and mushy.

Puree in blender and serve warm.

I first puréed apples to add to oatmeal, and that's when I realized that if you don't purée until smooth, it has just become the world's easiest applesauce! At certain groceries you can now purchase applesauce whose only ingredient is organic apples, so if you are short on time, simply purchase this applesauce ready-made. But this recipe helps to save all the energy and material used in manufacturing the packaging and then going in a landfill or being recycled.

What I like also is that I can make one serving at a time, choosing what type of apple to use. I like using Gala or Fuji apples, since they are a bit sweeter, but my son Oliver, who loves to suck on lemons, actually prefers the tart Granny Smith apples. (He must get some of his weirdness from his dad!)

Homemade Applesauce

Ingredients

2 Fuji apples (or variety of choice)
1/3 cup water
1/8 teaspoon cinnamon

Core and chop up apples, leaving peel on. Place in mini-processor. Add half the water and puree to desired texture, adding the remaining water only if necessary.

Add cinnamon and mix well.

Simply Avocado / Simply Banana

Ingredients

1 avocado

Taking a small pairing knife, slice around perimeter of avocado. Twist open. Use the blade of your knife to pull the pit out and discard.

Using a spoon, scoop out the flesh of the avocado into a bowl and mush with a fork. If you prefer, you can use your mini food processor instead. Of course, if your child has a few teeth, you can just spoon directly from the avocado without mashing.

Ingredients

1 banana

Ok, simply peel, place meat of the banana in a bowl, and mash with fork. Voila.

Again, if your child has a few teeth, you can cut the banana into very small bites, or let your child bite directly from the banana.

These recipes, if you even want to call them that, are so simple I'm almost embarrassed to include them. BUT, I had never eaten an avocado until I was in my 20s in California, so you never know!

Avocados and bananas are both great portable foods. If you are taking your baby out and need to bring food, both of these are really easy. For example, if I am out running errands and the boys need a quick snack, I will literally pull over to the side of the road, sit between their car seats, and spoon feed them an avocado. It's also nice, once your children get a bit older, that you can just let them bite directly off the banana. No, this picture isn't mashed potatoes, it's mashed banana and, yes, the other is mashed avo!

I think if I DIDN'T add this recipe, I would not be a true Ohioan! I know corn like the back of my hand since it was a staple growing up. When it's in season, this becomes one of my favorites because it's so sweet. Again, you can use breast milk or formula for familiarity. Make sure that it's thoroughly pureed so it's easier to digest. A little healthy tidbit about corn: according to the Whole Grain Council, corn has the highest level of antioxidants of any grain or vegetable – almost twice the antioxidant activity of apples!

Creamy Corn

Ingredients

1 ear corn
6 cups water
1/4 cup unsweetened almond or soy milk

Bring water to a boil and add ear of corn. Boil for 8 minutes. Remove ear and cut corn off ear.

Add corn to blender with milk and puree to smooth texture.

Serve warm.

Broccoli, Peas, and Pears Puree

Ingredients

1 cup chopped broccoli
1 cup peas
1 ripe pear
1/4 cup water

Place broccoli and water in a covered bowl. Microwave for about 4 minutes, until very soft.

Core the pear and add to blender along with the peas and cooked broccoli. Puree to desired texture, adding water if necessary.

Serve cool or room temperature.

This is a great puree to guarantee your baby gets his or her greens. And actually, like many babies, our boys like broccoli because it's a bit sweet. This is one of the few times I believe microwaving and water are a good way to cook . Steaming the broccoli (whether it's stove top or microwave) actually helps increase the special cholesterol-lowering benefits of the vegetable. The fiber-related components in the broccoli do a better job binding together the bile acids in your baby's digestive tract when they've been steamed. When this binding process takes place, it's easier for your baby's digestive system to get rid of the bile acids, resulting in the lowering of cholesterol.

Basic Apple Cinnamon Oatmeal

Ingredients

2 apples
1/2 cup steel cut oatmeal
1 1/4 cup water
cinnamon to taste

Bring water to boil and add oatmeal. Turn on low and cook for 30 minutes, stirring occasionally.

Core and cut apples, then puree to desired texture. Add to oatmeal. Mix in formula or breast milk to thin, if needed.

Sprinkle cinnamon in the cereal to taste.

For about two months straight, this is what our boys ate every night before bed. Some babies might not like the cinnamon, so try it on the side first.

You'll be glad to know that oats are filled with a cholesterol-lowering fiber called beta-glucan, as well as iron, a mineral that your body needs to carry oxygen to your muscles and other tissue. And with a total of four grams of fiber per half-cup, oatmeal helps your baby stay full longer, which means this doesn't need to be just for breakfast – a great night time meal as well, as our boys slept longer because they were full.

I love, love, love my crockpot! However, since I no longer use it for large pot roasts, having changed my diet philosophy, I had to get creative. I also know that I am NOT a morning person, so anything I can do to simplify my morning routines, I'm on board! Plus, there's nothing like prepping the boys' breakfast the night before . . . and waking up to the smell of breakfast already waiting for us. This 8-grain cereal usually contains oat bran, brown rice, corn, soybeans, millet, barley, sunflower seeds, and flaxseed—a great eight.

Crockpot 8 Grain Hot Cereal

Ingredients

4 cups unsweetened almond or soy milk, blended with 3 cups water
2 cups 8 grain hot cereal blended (I use Bob's Red Mill.)
2 cups blueberries
2 cups strawberries
1 teaspoon ground ginger
1/2 cup ground almonds
1 tablespoon olive oil

Coat the crockpot bowl with olive oil.

Combine milk and water with cereal right in the oiled bowl.

Separately, puree the blueberries, strawberries, ginger, and almonds. Stir this mixture into the crockpot and mix well with the cereal.

Cover and slow cook on LOW for 6-8 hours.

In the morning, dish into bowls. Freeze the rest. Easy to defrost and serve on other mornings when you just aren't feeling the cooking thing!

Mashed Cauliflower Puree

Ingredients

ChooseMyPlate.gov

2 large white cauliflowers
4 green onions, finely chopped
1 cup unsweetened almond or soy milk
1/2 clove garlic, finely sliced
1/4 teaspoon pepper
1 tablespoon olive oil

Preheat oven to 400 degrees.

Line a stock pot with the olive oil.

Clean and roughly chop up cauliflower and place in pot. Add green onions, garlic, pepper, and olive oil. Place a lid on the pot, and cook in oven for one hour or until cauliflower falls apart.

Place mixture in large bowl with 1/2 the milk, and mix with hand mixer, as you would for regular mashed potatoes if you want a chunky texture or place in blender for smoother texture. Don't use all the milk at once. Add it gradually to reach the texture of puree your baby desires.

Note: A lot of these recipes might seem thick. If the puree really is too thick, you can simply add water or another liquid, such as milk. Just remember it's much easier to thin a puree than it is to thicken it up.

This is a recipe that was inspired by a close friend of my mother's, Barbara Farrelly. When my mother had cancer and was going through her chemo, Barb would bring dinners over to our house for us. My mother always called vegetables "rabbit food," so our first reaction was "Eeew—mashed cauliflower." BUT, this was really one of those times when "don't knock it until you try it" never rang more true. It was so yummy even my mom loved it! (Ok, I have to admit the original recipe called for cream cheese and butter so Mom could tolerate it).

So, when I started making baby food, I couldn't think of a better puree to inspire me. Not all babies are open to green onions and garlic at first because these two foods are part of the "bitter" flavor family and can be a bit of an acquired taste. If your baby doesn't like these flavors, cut back on the amount of onions and garlic you add until your baby learns to appreciate them.

Turnip Cauliflower Puree

Ingredients

1 very large turnip
5 large carrots
1/2 head of average sized cauliflower
2 cups unsweetened almond or soy milk

Preheat oven to 400 degrees.

Peek skin off turnip and dice. Chop cauliflower and carrots.

Place all three ingredients in a dutch oven and cook for one hour.

Transfer to blender and puree, adding milk for texture.

Turnip season is fall/winter, cauliflower season is fall, and there is some type of carrot always in season year round, so fall would be the best time to have a crossover in vegetables. All the recipes in this book call for large carrots, but you can use baby carrots if your baby prefers a sweeter taste. However, please make sure that you purchase loose baby carrots and not the pre-packaged ones. Most processes for preparing pre-packaged baby carrots, as with most pre-packaged vegetables, include washing the vegetables in chlorine. This, combined with the packaging that clutters the environment, is the reason I buy my fruits and vegetables in bulk, not pre-packaged.

I like cooking my carrots in walnut oil because it gives a nice nutty flavor to them. My son, Oliver, is allergic to walnuts, but for some reason walnut oil is okay. However, if your child has a nut allergy, coconut oil works just fine in this recipe and it gives it a completely different flavor.

Rosemary Carrot Puree

Ingredients

10 large carrots
1 tablespoon ground rosemary
2 tablespoons walnut or coconut oil

Peel carrots and cut lengthwise into strips. Toss in a bowl with olive oil and ground rosemary – just enough to cover lightly, not soak them.

Place in a baking dish and cook at 350 degrees for 45 minutes or until very tender.

Add a bit of water and puree to reach the consistency you desire for your baby when under 12 months old. For older babies, no need to puree, simply serve as soft finger foods.

Beet and Sweet Potato Puree

Ingredients

1 large beet
1 large sweet potato
1/2 cup unsweetened almond or soy milk

Preheat oven to 400 degrees.

Scrub clean both the beet and the sweet potato, place both on cookie sheet, and bake for one hour or until tender when poked with a fork or knife. Remove from oven and remove the skin from the beet but not the skin from the sweet potato.

Place both in blender and puree, adding milk for a creamier texture.

Make sure <u>not</u> to remove the skin from the beet before cooking. And make sure <u>not</u> to puncture it because this causes a loss of both nutrients and flavor during the cooking process. Besides, it's a lot easier to remove the skin AFTER it's cooked.

Also make sure you leave the skin on the sweet potato. Lots of the nutrients are in the skin, so I leave it on. The blender can chop it fine enough that it becomes part of the puree.

Cauliflower, Leek, and Bean Puree

Ingredients

1 head cauliflowers
4 leeks
1 1/2 cups great northern beans, soaked, rinsed, cooked (or one 15 oz. can, drained and rinsed)
1 cup low sodium vegetable stock
1/4 teaspoon of nutmeg
pinch of pepper

Slice leeks lengthwise, clean, and cut into 1 inch pieces. Chop cauliflower.

Bring vegetable stock to a boil in an extra-large skillet, and then add leeks and cauliflower. Reduce heat to medium-low and simmer for 20 minutes or until tender.

Add beans, nutmeg, and pepper and cook for 5 more minutes. Puree mixture to desired texture.

When I make this recipe, I make about 8-10 cups of the great northern beans. After cooking them, I take only 1 1/2 cups out for this recipe, leaving the rest in the strainer and keeping in the fridge overnight to dry out so they don't freeze as one big clump. The next day, I fill an old bread bag full of the dried beans and then stick them in the freezer. When the boys want a finger food snack, I pull out however many beans I need and nuke them for only 30 seconds or until defrosted.

Potato Leek Puree

Ingredients

10 potatoes (I prefer Yukon, but you can use Russet)
3 large leeks
2 tablespoons olive oil
1 cup unsweetened almond or soy milk

Preheat oven to 400 degrees.

Scrub potatoes, and boil in a pot of water for 20 minutes or until tender.

Meanwhile, slice leeks lengthwise and rinse the insides to clean out all dirt. Cut the white part and the greenish-white part into 1 inch lengths.

Heat oil in a skillet on a medium-high heat, and saute the leeks for 10 minutes. Puree leeks and a 1/4 of the milk in a blender until smooth.

Drain potatoes and place in mixing bowl with remaining milk and mix with hand mixer, as you would for regular mashed potatoes if you want a chunky texture. If you want a smooth, runny texture, puree in a blender. Add leek and mix or puree to desired texture.

I love potato leek soup, so I thought, why not simplify it and see what the boys think? Sure enough, it is a hit! I think leeks make a great introduction to onions since they have a hint of that flavor but aren't quite as bold.

Leeks are also a great source of nutrition – high in vitamin C, potassium, bet-carotene, and folates. Translated, this means that they're great for your baby's heart, blood vessels, blood, and skin. Make sure that you puree the leeks smooth in this recipe before adding to the potatoes to guarantee smoothness. I prefer to use a hand mixer for the potatoes to keep a better consistency and then add the leeks at the end.

I know everyone has heard of superfoods, but I'm on a **superspice** kick! And turmeric is #1 on my list. It's most commonly found in Indian food, but I'm trying to find an excuse to use it in anything, such as a staple that I grew up with – mashed potatoes.

Turmeric has so many health benefits that include supporting your child's joint function, promoting beautiful skin (important to me since Oliver has eczema), and definitely helping digestion.

Indian Mashed Potatoes

Ingredients

1 lb. potatoes, washed, peeled and cubed
1 small yellow onion, finely chopped
1 cup unsweetened soy or almond milk
2 tablespoons olive oil
1/2 teaspoon mustard seeds
1/2 teaspoon cumin seeds
1/4 teaspoon black pepper
1/8 teaspoon turmeric

Bring a pot of water to boil and add potatoes. Boil about 20 minutes or until tender. Drain well, place in bowl, add milk, and use a hand mixer to desired texture just as you would regular mashed potatoes.

Meanwhile, finely crush the mustard seeds and cumin seeds using a mortar and pestle, or grind them up in a coffee grinder (make sure it's clean!).

Toss the above mixture with the black pepper, turmeric, onion, and olive oil in a large skillet and saute onions until slightly caramelized. Place in food processor until finely chopped.

Combine onions and potatoes, mix well, and serve warm.

 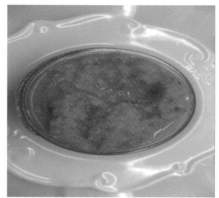

All the beans in these recipes can be prepped two ways, canned or dried. The advantage of canned beans comes when you are in a hurry or simply have limited time (or you are just plain exhausted!). Canned beans are as easy as opening the can and rinsing.

Dried beans are much more laborious, yes. But there are so many more advantages. For example, it is MUCH less expensive to buy beans in bulk, dried beans are much more lightweight (no cans to transport), and they create very little packaging waste – so much better for the environment. So, for a recipe like this one, I will buy about 3 pounds of bulk chickpeas, put them in a pot of water before I go to bed, and let them soak for 12 hours. The next day, I drain the water, rinse, and start boiling them for about an hour or until tender. I do this before I feed the boys breakfast, so that by the time I am finished dressing and feeding them, the beans are about ready. I then keep them in the strainer in the sink for a couple hours so that they dry out a bit, and then I freeze them in a leftover bread bag. Then, fixing other recipes like this one become a cinch because I just pull out as many beans as the recipe calls for.

Chickpea Puree

Ingredients

1 large green zucchini, diced
1 large yellow bottleneck squash, diced
1 cup cooked chickpeas
2 large heirloom tomatoes, diced
1 tablespoon olive oil

Add the diced zucchini, squash, and tomatoes to the skillet with olive oil and saute on medium heat for 10 minutes.

Add chickpeas and cook on medium-low heat for another 10 minutes.

Puree to desired texture.

Banana, Strawberry, and Brown Rice Puree

Ingredients

2 bananas
1 cup strawberries
1 cup brown rice
2 1/2 cups water

Bring water to a boil and add rice. Cover and simmer for 40-50 minutes. Remove from heat and let sit for an additional 10 minutes and fluff with fork.

Place rice, strawberries, and bananas to blender and puree until smooth.

An easy way to make your own puree is to think about what flavor combinations you appreciate. For example, when I purchase smoothies when I'm out and about, I tend to order the strawberry banana combo. So, why not make it into a puree? Adding brown rice not only thickens it up, but adds nutrients such as fiber and selenium, which is great for your baby's immune system.

Cherry Apple Puree

Ingredients

1 cup cherries
3 apples

Wash and pit cherries. Wash, core, and slice apples.

Place all ingredients in blender and puree until smooth.

This is a typical all-American recipe - apple pie or cherry pie? Nope, puree! This is a great example that simple fruit can be a great dessert for your child with no processed crust or added sugar. But, I promise you, just as sweet and delicious for your baby. Now that I live in the Pacific Northwest, I love making this easy recipe with Washington apples and Rainier cherries in the summer - yum!

"Make sure you eat your fruits and veggies!" That's what I hear from the doctor. Well, this recipe gets to the heart of it and I mean that literally. Not only do the peas and pears provide fiber, but the spinach provides vitamin C, folate, potassium, and magnesium to help prevent cardiovascular disease. I like using baby spinach because I think it's a bit sweeter. Because you are pureeing the entire meal, you can don't have to destem the spinach – just throw it in!

Peas, Pears, and Spinach Puree

Ingredients

1 cup peas
1 pear, sliced with skin on
1/2 cup baby spinach

Combine all ingredients in a food
processor and blend until smooth.

I had never HEARD of lentils, let alone ate any, until about year ago. Now that I am working towards a healthier lifestyle, I don't know how I went so long without them! They are now a staple in our household since they are so high in protein and an incredible source of iron! While this recipe is more work than, say pureed bananas, it quickly became one of my boys' favorites and I make extra to freeze for later. I love adding lots of almond milk to it and making a soup for my lunch too!

Cauliflower Lentil Puree

Ingredients

1 cup red lentils
2 leeks, sliced
2 yams, diced
1 half head of cauliflower florets, finely chopped
32 oz. low sodium vegetable stock
2 apples, cored and chopped

Bring vegetable stock to a boil in extra large saucepan.

Add all cleaned and cut ingredients to vegetable stock and lower temperature to low-medium heat. Cover and cook for 30-45 minutes, stirring occasionally. When cauliflower and yams are tender, remove from heat.

Puree in blender, adding water or almond milk if necessary for desired texture.

Green Peach Smoothie

Ingredients

3 peaches
3 bananas
3 pears
1 cup baby spinach
16 oz almond, soy, or coconut yogurt

Slice fruits, removing seeds or pits as needed.

Place all ingredients in a blender or food processor and puree until desired texture is achieved.

Anytime I make a smoothie for the boys, I make extra because I love to enjoy the treat too! The spinach might not sound appetizing, but the sweetness of the fruit really masks the flavor of the spinach.

If you like to add more protein to your child's diet, substitute soy yogurt instead because soy has more protein than almond or coconut yogurt.

Peach Blueberry Tofu Mash

Ingredients

1/2 cup wild blueberries
1 large peach, pitted and diced
1/2 package of firm tofu (usually about 7 oz)

Combine all of the above ingredients in a blender.

Add water if needed and puree.

Tofu and fruit are great beginner foods for your baby. Picking any good combination of fruit brings flavor to the tofu, so this recipe can change depending on the season of the fruit at your local farmer's market. Actually, choosing fruit that is in season is not only better for the environment, but also easier on your pocketbook. The harder to find, the higher the price. Blueberry season can be as early as May and usually ends in late summer. Peaches are also a summer fruit. If you want to change this recipe up for the winter time, just substitute oranges, pears, or persimmons.

Did you say pudding when you read this recipe's title? Read again! I said puddin'. That's how I grew up saying it, and some things shouldn't change.

This is a SUPER easy recipe that I find hard <u>not</u> to eat myself. I think using an actual vanilla bean gives more flavor and is more natural, but I'm also quite aware that most people stock vanilla extract in their pantries rather than vanilla beans. If you want to substitute extract, just translate the recipe's 1 inch of vanilla bean into 1 teaspoon of extract.

Chia Seed Puddin'

Ingredients

2 cups unsweetened almond or soy milk
3/4 cup chia seeds
1 inch vanilla bean, scraped clean

Combine all the ingredients in a large bowl and whisk vigorously. (Or, put the ingredients in your Kitchen Aid mixer with a whisk attachment for about 2-3 minutes.) If your child is old enough, the best is to place all ingredients in a Mason jar with its lid on tight and let your child shake it up.

Place container in the fridge overnight to allow the mixture to thicken to a puddin' texture as the chia seeds absorb the mixture.

Serve chilled, adding any pureed fruit if desired.

Butternut Squash Puree

Ingredients

1 extra large butternut squash
1 cup unsweetened almond or soy milk
1/2 teaspoon nutmeg
1 tablespoon olive oil

Preheat oven to 400. Brush baking pan with olive oil.

Cut squash in half lengthwise, place open face down on pan, and bake for 50 minutes or until soft.

Remove from oven and scoop out seeds. Scoop flesh away from skin and puree with milk to desired texture.

I think I could write an entire cookbook just using butternut squash! It is such a well-rounded vegetable in flavor and nutrients. It's highest in Vitamin A, a great anti-oxidant that helps maintain your skin, eyesight and helps the body protect against certain cancers such as lung and oral cavity cancers! But, for now I'll keep the vegetable simple. You can make this puree with or without the nutmeg since both are delicious!

Strawberry Rhubarb Quinoa Puree

Ingredients

1 2/3 cup water
1 stalk rhubarb
2 cups strawberries
1/2 cup quinoa

Wash and cut rhubarb into one inch pieces. Bring 2/3 cup
water to a boil, add rhubarb, and cook for 10 minutes. The rhubarb should be soft and stringy.
Cut tops off strawberries and place in blender.

Meanwhile, bring 1 cup water to boil and add quinoa. Cover and simmer for 20 minutes.

When rhubarb and quinoa are finished cooking, combine with strawberries in blender and puree.

Serve warm or chilled.

When I think summertime, I think strawberry rhubarb pie – one of my dad's favorites. If you take away all the sugar and go back to the basics, this puree becomes a healthy dessert treat. Most desserts that include rhubarb you will notice added sugar because rhubarb tends to have a tart taste. However, the sweetness of the strawberries makes this a perfect beginner sweet combo for your child.

Otherwise known as "The Clean Out Puree"! Apples help the digestive tract with fiber and the prunes, well, clean ya out! Make sure that you introduce it slowly since prunes are powerful. And have some extra diapers ready. But in all seriousness, prunes pack in calcium, vitamin k, and the B vitamins, and babies love this because it's super sweet!

Prune Apple Puree

Ingredients

10 prunes
1 medium size red apple

Place in blender and puree until smooth.

Serve at room temperature or chilled.

Banana Walnut Cereal

Ingredients

ChooseMyPlate.gov

3 cups water
1 cup 8 grain cereal
2 small bananas
1/2 cup walnuts
1/2 cup raisins
1/2 cup **unsweetened almond or soy milk**

Bring water to boil and add cereal and raisins. Cover and simmer for 10 minutes.

Meanwhile, add banana and walnuts to food processor and blend until smooth.

When cereal is finished, stir in banana and walnut mixture
and milk to desired texture.

If you ever want to be depressed with the direction of our children's nutrition, just take a stroll down the cereal aisle at the grocery. So many of the cereals are marketed to kids with fun cartoon pictures and chocked full of processed grains, artificial colors, and added sugars. Nip this horrible habit in the bud and start your baby on healthy foods at a young age. Don't even go down the aisle with your child! They only know what is taught to them. Teach them the yummiest features of whole grains and real fruit. This delicious breakfast meal gets your baby off to the right start of the day! By the way, I think walnuts taste better in this recipe, but I substitute almonds since one of my children is allergic to walnuts. If your baby is allergic to all nuts, just exclude them completely.

Chia Seed and Banana Puree

Ingredients

2 bananas
1 tablespoon chia seeds
1 cup unsweetened almond or soy milk
1/2 cup barley
2 1/2 cups water

Soak chia seeds in almond or breast milk in fridge for 6-8 hours or until soft.

In a small pan, bring water to boil, add barley, and cook for 50-60 minutes or until soft.

Place banana, barley, chia seeds and any extra liquid in blender and puree to smooth texture.

Did you know that your brain is 60% fat and that all brain cells are produced by the time you are two? This is one reason why companies push whole milk - it has lots of fat. This is a great recipe to get the healthy Omega-3 fatty acids needed for brain development from Chia seeds instead. I call this recipe Brain Food!

Beans 'n Rice

Ingredients

1 tablespoon olive oil
1 small yellow onion, finely chopped
1 green pepper, cored, seeded, finely chopped
1 sweet red pepper, cored, seeded, finely chopped
1 large zucchini, finely diced
4 cups cooked red kidney beans (or 2 15-oz. cans red kidney beans, drained, rinsed)
2 large heirloom tomatoes, chopped
3/4 teaspoon ground cumin
3/4 teaspoon ground cinnamon
3/4 cup raisins
2 cups wild rice
4 1/2 cups water
1/4 cup chopped scallion
zest of 1 lime

Heat oil in a large skillet over medium-high heat. Add onion, peppers, and zucchini,x and cook for 5 minutes. Stir in beans, tomatoes, cumin, and cinnamon. Simmer for 5 minutes. Stir in raisins.

Meanwhile, bring water to a boil and add wild rice. Cover and cook on low, stirring occasionally, for 1 1/2 hours or until tender. Stir in scallion, lime zest. When finished, add all other ingredients and mix well.

Serve warm.

This recipe is packed full of protein between the beans and, would you guess, wild rice? Wild rice is a great source of not just protein, but also fiber, iron, vitamin B6, and potassium. And it's gluten free! Last, the tomatoes contains Lycopene, an antioxidant compound, which gives them their beautiful colors. It's good for your heart and your eyes, and some would even say it helps prevent certain cancers. Lycopene is fat-soluble, which means your baby will absorb more of it by cooking the tomatoes in a healthy fat, like the olive oil in this recipe! You can use any type of tomato. I like using heirloom tomatoes in this recipe because they usually have more juice that can saturate the rice with more flavor.

Pasta Marinara

Ingredients

2 cups (16-oz. package) whole wheat organic orzo
10 white button mushrooms, sliced
3 large heirloom tomatoes, diced
3 cups baby spinach
2 basil leaves
2 tablespoons olive oil
1 cup great northern beans, cooked

Bring water to boil and cook orzo for 8 minutes or until tender. Place in large bowl.

In a large saucepan, sauté mushrooms, tomatoes, baby spinach, great northern beans, and basil in olive oil for 15 minutes on medium heat. Transfer to food processor and blend to desired texture.

Mix with orzo and serve warm.

I have a horrible green thumb. Somehow I even managed to kill a cactus once. But, this past summer I noticed at the grocery a whole basil plant for $3.99. I walked past it until I realized in the produce department that I was about to purchase a small container of basil for the same price. So I thought if I could even get two servings' worth of basil out of this little plant, I'll have saved a container from going into a landfill, **and** I'll have saved $3.99. I'm so proud of myself — that little basil plant gets absolutely no love, and it's still going strong. So, even if you don't think you can do it, just pick ONE herb and try it out!

Now to orzo, another ingredient listed. Orzo is fun to work with because, while it looks like rice, it's actually a pasta. It's a great size for introducing pasta to babies, so I use it in a lot of my cooking. This is such an easy recipe that my boys love, and so do I, so it is definitely served often in our house.

And did you know that whole wheat pasta is considered a whole grain? According to the American Society for Clinical Nutrition, eating three or more servings of whole grains — such as whole-wheat pasta — each day can possibly lessen your risk of Type 2 diabetes. This is because the beneficial effect of soluble fiber might be increased through the slow absorption and digestion of the whole grains – which can help reduce the demand for insulin.

Every time you walk into the grocery, you face a daunting task: How do I pick the healthiest, most nutrient-packed foods for your baby, and how do I see past all the attractive, colorful packaging and all the deceptive claims? My brother-in-law, Aric, gave me some wonderful and simple advice to make grocery shopping easier: "Shop the perimeter of the grocery. Most processed foods are in the middle aisles, and the healthier foods are along the walls." It really is true! Even down to buying canned potatoes versus the real thing. Why create packaging waste when I can buy fresh? Try it out the next time you are at the grocery!

Split Pea and Sweet Potato Mash

Ingredients

4 cups low-sodium vegetable stock
1 cup water
2 1/2 cups dry split peas
1/2 small onion, finely chopped
2 large sweet potatoes, diced
4 ribs celery, diced
1 cup finely chopped kale
1 teaspoon dried oregano
1/4 teaspoon cumin
1/8 teaspoon celery seed

Fill a large pot with the vegetable stock, water, and split peas, and bring to a boil. Turn down to a low-medium boil – not a simmer – and cook for 30 minutes, stirring occasionally.

Grind the spices in a mortar and pestle or a clean coffee grinder. Add all the remaining ingredients and cook on medium heat for another 30 minutes or until potatoes are soft.

Stir well and serve warm.

Cherry Quinoa

Ingredients

2 cups water
3/4 cup quinoa
3 inches vanilla bean (or 3 teaspoons vanilla extract)
1 to 2 teaspoons finely shredded orange peel
1/2 cup almonds
1/2 cup cherries, chopped

Bring water to a boil and stir in the quinoa and orange peel, then remove pan from heat. Cover and let stand for 20 minutes.

Meanwhile, grind the almonds in your food processor or in a coffee grinder (a completely clean one!).

Fluff the couscous with a fork. Stir in the almond grinds and the cherries.

Serve warm.

Cherries are in season during the summer, so this makes a fun start to a summer day or as an afternoon dessert. Either way, my boys love this one and it's a great source of protein due to the quinoa. That is why I have used the quinoa on the nutrition plate as a grain AND protein source!

Avocado is one of my kids' favorite foods, so any recipe that incorporates avocado is a winner in their book! Avocados are a super food for a baby's diet because they contain such a great fat content, which is critical for healthy brain development. This recipe is wonderful because it's a well rounded meal and is a great source of protein due to the beans. Any bean can suffice, but pinto has the most flavor for my kids in this recipe. Also, only add the avocado to what you serve immediately because it turns brown quickly when stored.

Avocado, Beans, and Rice

Ingredients

3 cups water
1 cup brown rice
1 avocado, pitted and finely diced
1 Roma tomato, finely diced
1/2 cup pinto beans, cooked
2 tablespoons olive oil or avocado oil

Bring water to a boil and add brown rice. Cover and simmer for 40 minutes.

Add tomato, beans, and oil and simmer for an additional 10 minutes.

Stir in avocado just as you are serving.

Squash "Spaghetti"

Ingredients

1 large spaghetti squash
2 cups green sweet peas
1/2 tablespoon nutmeg
1/2 teaspoon pepper

Preheat oven to 375 degrees.

Spread olive oil over baking sheet.

Slice squash lengthwise, and place face down on the baking sheet. Bake for 1 hour.

When cool enough to handle, scoop the seeds and fibrous strings from the center. Then scrape around the edge of the squash with the tines of a fork to shred the pulp into strands.

Place the shredded strands in a bowl. Add peas, nutmeg, and pepper.

Serve warm.

I confess: I discovered spaghetti squash by accident. It was mixed in with the acorn squash at the store, and I thought it had to be similar, so what the heck. After I baked it like my acorn squash, I was so confused as to the shredding, so I just pureed it for the boys. Which, by the way, is GREAT with a dash of pumpkin allspice. But then I did a bit of homework and learned that the real beauty of this vegetable is that it is commonly used as an alternative to pasta. Makes sense, right? Hence the name. So, here's a new dish I now make for the boys. This squash is available year-round, but its peak season is in the fall.

I used to buy fresh edamame, but I spent more time squeezing those sweet little things out of the pod than I did sleeping, I swear! And while I hate contributing to consumer packaging, I confess that I cut corners a bit by buying organic shelled edamame in the frozen package form.

Edamame is another almost perfect food because it's a great source of protein. Our boys love to eat them as a snack as it was one of their first finger-dexterity foods.

Cranberry Edamame Couscous

Ingredients

1 cup couscous
1 1/2 cup water
2 tablespoons olive oil
2 teaspoon fresh lemon juice
1 cup shelled edamame
1/2 cup dried cranberries

Bring water to a boil in a small pot. Add couscous, remove from heat, and cover for 10 minutes.

Fluff couscous and stir in remaining ingredients.

Serve warm or cool.

I have to admit, this one might be an acquired taste. Personally, I am not a fan of Swiss chard, but it's really hard to ignore the nutritional benefits that make this a super food. The first time I had Swiss chard was when I was visiting a friend of mine, Nikki Cerra, and she made scrambled eggs with mushrooms and Swiss chard. Thankfully, we are close enough friends that I felt completely comfortable spitting it out immediately and asking her why she was trying to kill me. She proceeded to tell me about how wonderful it was, but the whole time I was taking the information in, I was still wondering if it would be rude to excuse myself and go brush my teeth 15 times. To this day, I am still working on it, but in the meantime, I'm shocked to find that my sons actually like the stuff. Go figure! So, here's a recipe certainly not for the faint of heart...

Garlic Swiss Chard

Ingredients

2 pounds Swiss chard (red or rainbow)
2 tablespoons olive oil
1/2 clove garlic, sliced

Remove stems from chard and discard. Finely chop the chard leaves.

In a large skillet, heat olive oil over medium heat. Add garlic and cook 1 to 2 minutes, being careful not to burn garlic.

Stir in chard leaves and cook for another **4 minutes**, stirring occasionally with tongs.

Serve warm.

Black Bean & Sweet Potato Scramble

Ingredients

1/2 small yellow onion, finely chopped
3 teaspoons dried thyme leaves, crushed
4 to 5 tablespoons olive oil
1 sweet red pepper, finely chopped
1 green pepper, finely chopped
1 extra large sweet potato, cut into very small cubes
2 cups cooked black beans (or one 15 oz can black beans, drained and rinsed)
pepper to taste

In large skillet, sauté onion and thyme in oil until onion is tender, about 5 minutes.

Add red pepper and sweet potatoes; sauté until potatoes begin to soften, about 8 minutes.

Stir in beans, and cook until potatoes are tender, about 5 minutes.

Season with pepper to taste.

Did you know that thyme is loaded with iron? And that iron is critical for growing children, especially when they are eating a plant-based diet? Well, now you know. Also, thyme is rich in manganese, a mineral that boosts brain function and helps make healthy bones — all very important for your children at such a critical age. So, if your kids like the taste, add as much as they desire. You can't overdose on thyme!

Quinoa Stir Fry

Ingredients

1 cup quinoa
1 apple
1 yellow squash
1 zucchini
1 red pepper
3 tablespoons coconut oil

Bring 2 cups water to a boil, then add 1 cup quinoa. Remove from burner and cover. Let sit for about 20 minutes to let quinoa completely absorb the water.

Finely dice the apple, squash, zucchini, and red pepper.

Melt coconut oil in a skillet on medium high heat, and add all the diced ingredients. Cook for about 10 minutes or until all ingredients are tender.

Pour quinoa into a mixing bowl and fluff. Add the cooked diced ingredients and mix well.

Serve warm or cool.

I am a bit infatuated with coconut oil. In our household it has purpose way beyond just cooking. For example, most people who know our family also know we us it for diaper cream too! (yes, a different container – eww.) When the boys were first born, I didn't like putting diaper cream chemicals on my newborns. When Oliver was in the NICU (Neonatal Intensive Care Unit), a nurse recommended using food-grade organic coconut oil. And so my addiction began. My boys now have the shiniest, yummiest-smelling tushies in town!

I could go on and on about the other uses for coconut oil, but that's another book, another day. In the meantime, enjoy it in this yummy recipe.

Farro with Edamame, Peas, and Mushrooms

Ingredients

1 tablespoon olive oil
1/3 cup chopped small yellow onion
1 cup farro
3 cups water
1 cup edamame
1 cup fresh peas
1 cup finely chopped white button mushrooms

Bring water to a boil and add farro. Cook on medium-low heat for 40 minutes, stirring occasionally until farro is tender.

Meanwhile, heat oil in a large saucepan on medium heat. Add the onions and mushrooms. Cook and stir for 5 minutes or until tender. Add the peas and edamame and stir to heat through.

Combine all ingredients, stir well, and serve warm.

Farro is a great alternative to rice for variety of flavor and texture and contains great disease fighting antioxidants. This makes a great dish that includes a protein, a starch, and a vegetable! There are different ways to cook farro. If I know I won't have much time to make this, I'll throw the farro in a pot of water before I go to bed. Then, the next day, I'll rinse the farro, shortening the cooking time to only 10-15 minutes and cutting the amount of vegetable broth in half. Note, however, that cooking farro for a shorter time results in a more chewy texture, while a longer cooking time results in a mushier texture. So, depending on the age of your children and their taste preference, adjust the cooking times accordingly.

Here's another great breakfast food that you can prep the night before. Wheat berries will require rinsing and soaking first. I recommend that you do this in the morning, so in the evening they are ready to go into your crockpot.

Cranberry Almond Wheat Berries

Ingredients

ChooseMyPlate.gov

1 teaspoon olive oil
4 cups unsweetened almond milk
1 1/2 cup wheat berries
1 cup water
3 red apples, cored and pureed
1/3 cup old-fashioned steel cut oatmeal
1 inch stripped vanilla bean
1 teaspoon ground cinnamon
1/4 cup ground almonds
6 tablespoons cranberries

Coat the inside of a 4-5 1/2 quart crockpot with olive oil.

Combine almond milk, wheat berries, water, apples, oats, almonds, and cinnamon in prepared slow cooker.

Cover and slow cook on LOW for 9 hours. Uncover and stir in cranberries. Serve warm.

Index

If you like what you read and are craving more:

freshstartcookbook.com